अंग काव्य

---

ang kavya

अंग काव्य

Nomenclature for hand movements and feet positions in Kathak

ang kavya

by

Pt. Birju Maharaj

HAR-ANAND
PUBLICATIONS PVT LTD

Har-Anand Publications Pvt Ltd
E-49/3, Okhla Industrial Area, Phase-2, New Delhi-110020
Tel.: 41603491
E-mail: haranand@rediffmail.com / info@haranandbooks.com
Shop online at: www.haranandbooks.com

 @haranand_publications

Har Anand Publications

Reprint, 2026

Credits :

Photographs by : Avinash Pasricha
Text by : Saswati Sen
Drawings by : Raghava R. Bhatt
Page make-up by : Surender Sejwal

Printed in India
Published by Ashok Gosain and Ashish Gosain for Har-Anand Publications Pvt Ltd
and printed in India at Royal Press

॥ कथा कहे सो कथिक कहावे ॥

This phrase gradually took shape in a beautiful form - Kathak, the story-telling tradition of the temples of north India. From the rustic cloth bag of the village minstrel, it travelled through the royal courts of Hindu and Muslim rulers and finally reached the proscenium stage, as one of the foremost classical dance forms of India. Like the other forms, this too was basically passed on as an oral tradition from guru to shishya with very little material available as written text.

Today, times have changed, and a standard, codified nomenclature is a felt need in imparting training to students.

Pt. Birju Maharaj, the living legend who has been central to the renaissance of Kathak today, particularly contributing to its aesthetic richness, has meticulously given names for every abstract hand movement (nritta hastaka) and foot position (pada bhangima). To further make it easy to refer to and communicate, these movements have been codified into a 'dance shorthand' which would greatly facilitate documentation. In addition to the major lines representing the upper arm, forearm and wrist, a tiny dot has also been used to identify the direction of the palm. The main syllables corresponding to the movements have also been mentioned.

This will be the first book of its kind, and is expected to be of great value to Kathak students all over the world.

Contents

Hand movements

मूल Basic

उत्पत्ति  utpatti

Both hands brought near chest center, first finger tip and thumb touching each other, palms facing downward. Almost all nritta hastakas start from this position.

नमन naman

Both hands in loosely clasped position, 6 inches in front of chest center, right palm over left. This is the main position of the hands for footwork.

पलट 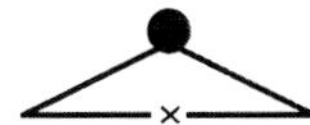 palat

Turning the palm over with the rotation of the wrist.

स्थिर

sthira

One hand remains at utpatti position, the other extends firmly on one side of the body, palm facing down.

ऊर्ध्व हस्त चक्र

urdhva hasta chakra

The hand moves upward from utpatti with fingertips drooping down; fingers open outward towards audience as palm faces up, wrist rotates in a half circle (clockwise for left and anti clockwise for right) as if holding a plate, then hand glides down palm facing audience, back to utpatti.

ta thei thei tat

मध्य हस्त चक्र  madhya hasta chakra

Hand moves forward and outward, palm facing up,
then gradually travels sideways, tracing a circular path,
returning to utpatti position.

ta thei thei tat

तल हस्त चक्र 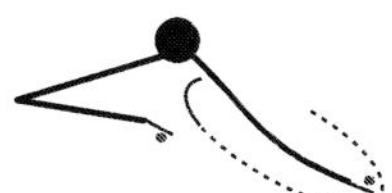 tala hasta chakra

(Right) Wrist rolls down in front, palm facing audience, arm fully extended, then swings downward and backward as palm faces out, finally pulling back to utpatti position as wrist turns in an anti-clockwise half circle.

ta thei thei tat

ऊर्ध्व कोण सूचिता  urdhva kona suchita

Hand travels from utpatti position diagonally upward,
as palm snaps open with a sharp jerk, facing up.

thei

मध्य कोण सूचिता  madhya kona suchita

Hand moves out from utpatti position, extends fully (shoulder level height), finger tips pointing out, palm facing up.

thei

तल कोण सूचिता  tala kona suchita

Arm moves from utpatti position downward, snapping open in full extension (palm facing up).

thei

समतल  samatal

Arm moves away from body, fully extended to the side
at shoulder level height (palm facing down).

tat

Both arms open sideways outward and move forward as if in an embrace.
The rotation of wrist is important.

ta thei tat

Both arms extend in front, then move to the sides (palm up)
and return to utpatti position.

tig dha dig dig

अर्धालिंगन  ardhaalingan

Arm extends to the side, encircles forward and pulls back to utpatti position
(wrist position important)

ta thei tat

पुष्पक pushpak

Both hands move straight up, palms touch each other at base of thumb mound, make a complete twist rotation as they come down to utpatti position.

Hand movements

शृंगारिक Ornamental

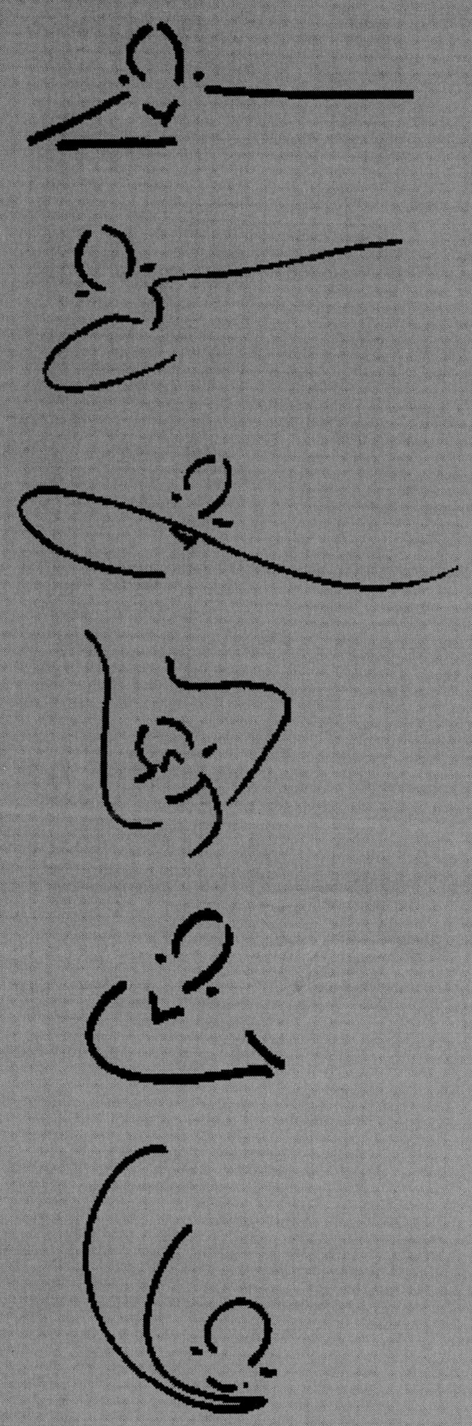

प्रवाह   pravaaha

One arm extends to the side, the other points in that direction but remains near chest center; wrists rotate in opposite direction moving from out to in.

लयशिखा lavashikha

Wrists rotate in opposite directions as one arm extends diagonally upward and forward and the other arm goes exactly opposite, downward.

ta thei ta ta thei

थाप

thaap

Arm extends outward and palm snaps as if slapping on a drum.

dha

स्वागत  swaagat

Both arms extend on one side (palm upwards), as if to welcome, then pull back as elbows are bent.

ta ka

Both palms are cupped, with the little fingers of each touching each other.

thun

मतंग matang

Both hands move out from utpatti position: one going upwards, the other downwards diagonally opposite, then the wrist turns and they stop with a jerk, palms facing out.

उमंग  umang

Both hands go up as the wrist rolls from inside and opens with palms facing out.

thung ta

ध्वज.  dhvaja

The wrists roll from inside as both hands go up and fingers point towards the corner (palms facing audience).

tho

स्रोत 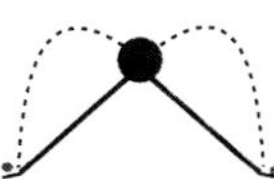 srota

Both hands move upward (till forehead level), fingers tapering down; then sharply move down and fall on both sides of the body, (about 12 inches away), palms facing outward.

tat tat

अर्धांग  ardhaanga

The palm near the chest in Sthira Hastak, is held fully erect upwards, facing sideways and out.

theiya

Hand movements

चक्कर Circles

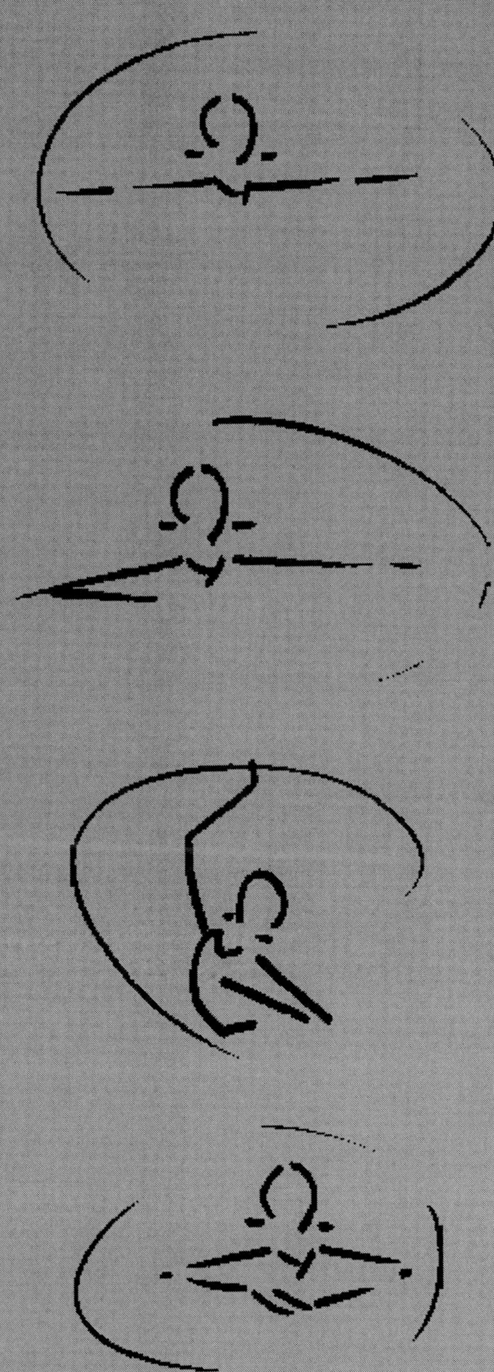

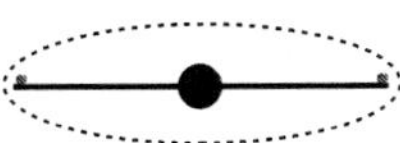

Both arms stretch out almost sideways as the body starts to rotate (mostly anti-clockwise) on an axis, then return back to utpatti position as the turn is completed.

tig dha dig dig

अर्धफेरी  ardhapheri

Each arm stretches out alternately and is pulled back, as the body makes half rotations back and forth on its axis.

tig dha dig dig

बद्धफेरी

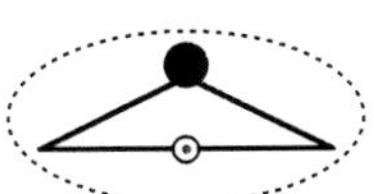

baddhapheri

The body spins (anti-clockwise) as the hands remain either in utpatti position or are held together at the calves.

मुक्तफेरी muktapheri

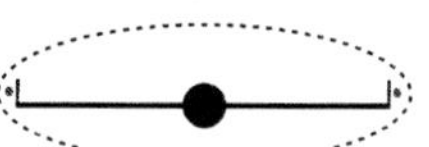

As the body completes each spin, the arms open from central utpatti position and stretch to the sides, palms facing out.

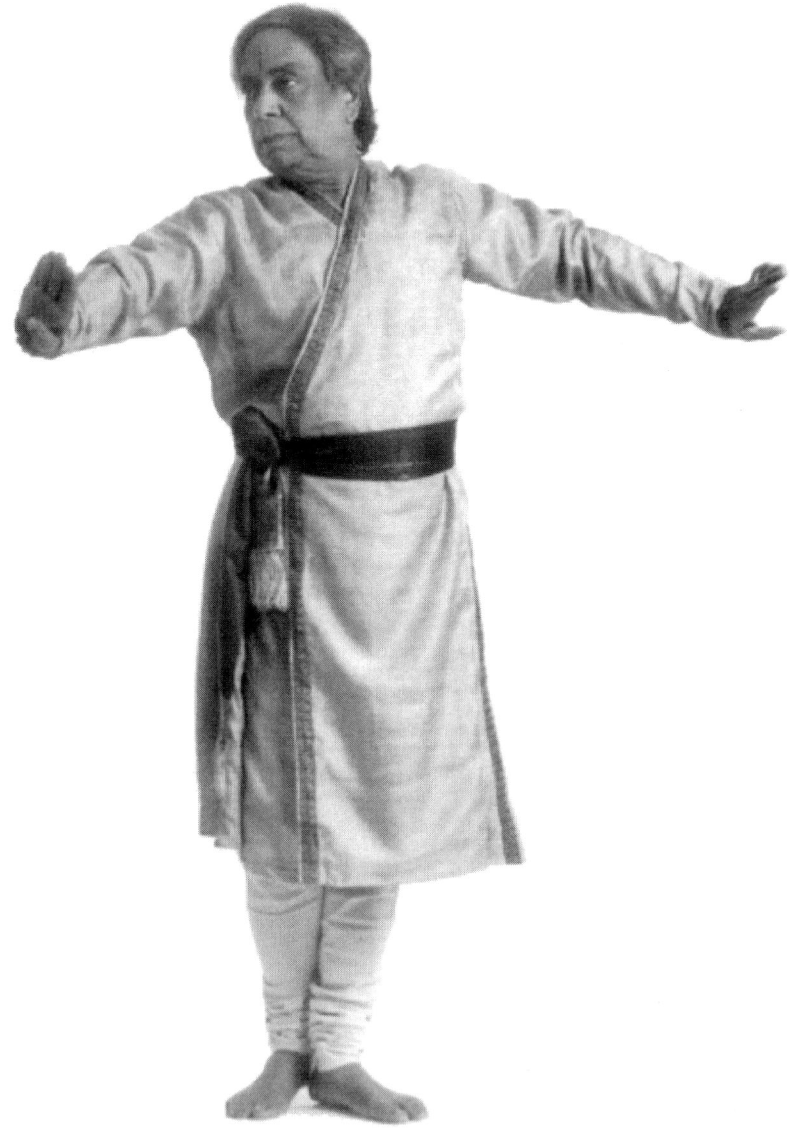

tig dha dig dig

पवनफेरी

pavanpheri

As the body starts to spin (anti-clockwise), the right hand opens in front and is pulled back simultaneously as the left hand moves upward, the wrist rotating above the head like Urdhva Hasta Chakra, before coming down with the completion of the spin.

tat tat thei

Hand movements

कलास विशेष Wrist emphases

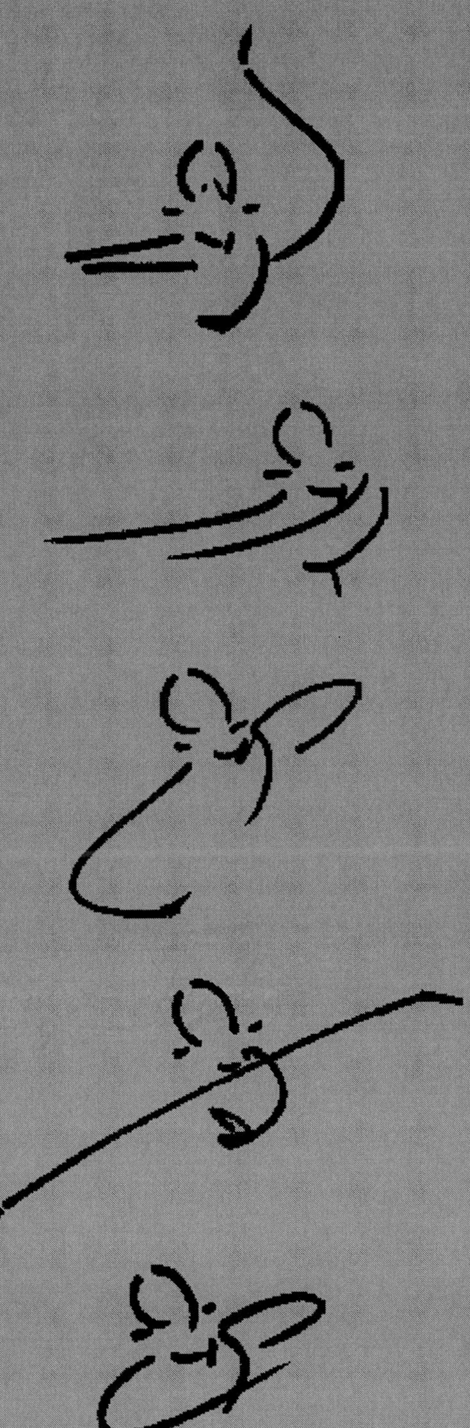

चपल कलास

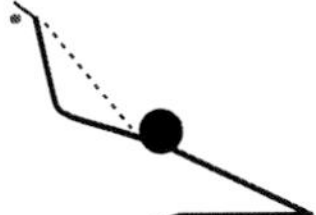

chapal kalaas

One or both arms go back and forth from utpatti position upward, with the palm facing out.
The sideways flip turn of the wrist is important.

thei thei ta

Brisk jerks (sideways) are made at the wrist joint.

thei thei

जलभ्रमरी  jalbhramari

Hand moves down and makes a circular movement at waist level,
as wrist rotates from inside moving outward as if balancing a plate on the palm.
(Sometimes this movement is done as the body turns).

she she

Both hands snap at the wrists, as if striking a big drum (dholak/pakhawaj) from both ends.

dhit tam

Hand extends out gracefully upto the point when a scoop or bow shape of the arm is obtained (palm facing upward).

Notation symbols (feet)

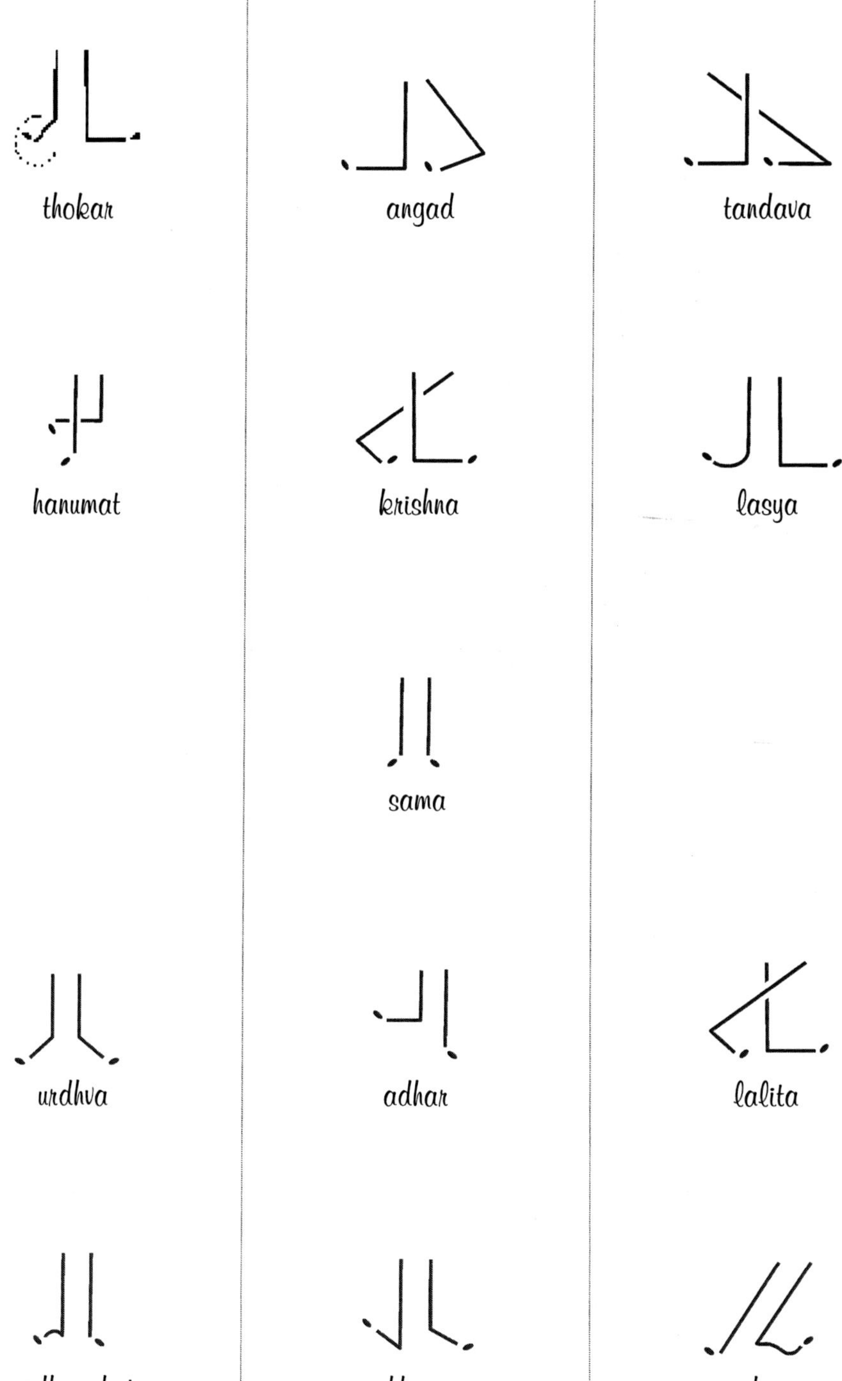

Hand extends out gracefully upto the point when a scoop or bow shape of the arm is obtained (palm facing upward).

tat

कवच  kavach

One hand comes near the opposite side of the waist, (about 6 inches from it) as the body twists and bends toward that waist. Mostly used while starting 'Gat'.

पलटा 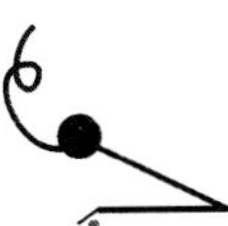 paltaa

Hand moves upwards from Kavach position, wrist encircles over head (palm upward) as body makes a complete turn, then returns to utpatti. Always used to start a 'Gat'. Usually one hand follows the other, as the body turns back and forth as if unwinding.

ta thei thei

चंवर 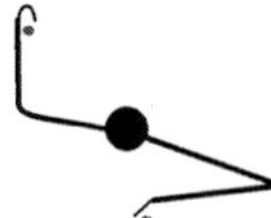 chavar

The hand moves upward, fingers pointing down and stops as palm flips out gracefully. This movement is very similar to Urdhva Kona Suchita except for its soft and graceful execution.

tat tat thei

अर्पण  arpan

Both hands extend downwards almost parallel to each other, palms facing outward (the feeling is that of offering).

thei

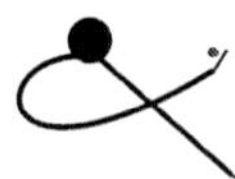

The hand sweeps up from Sthira position, travelling upto the opposite shoulder level, then the wrist turns so that the palm faces oneself (as if to see a mirror).

Both hands circle over the head, tracing a parallel path.

Notation symbols (hands)

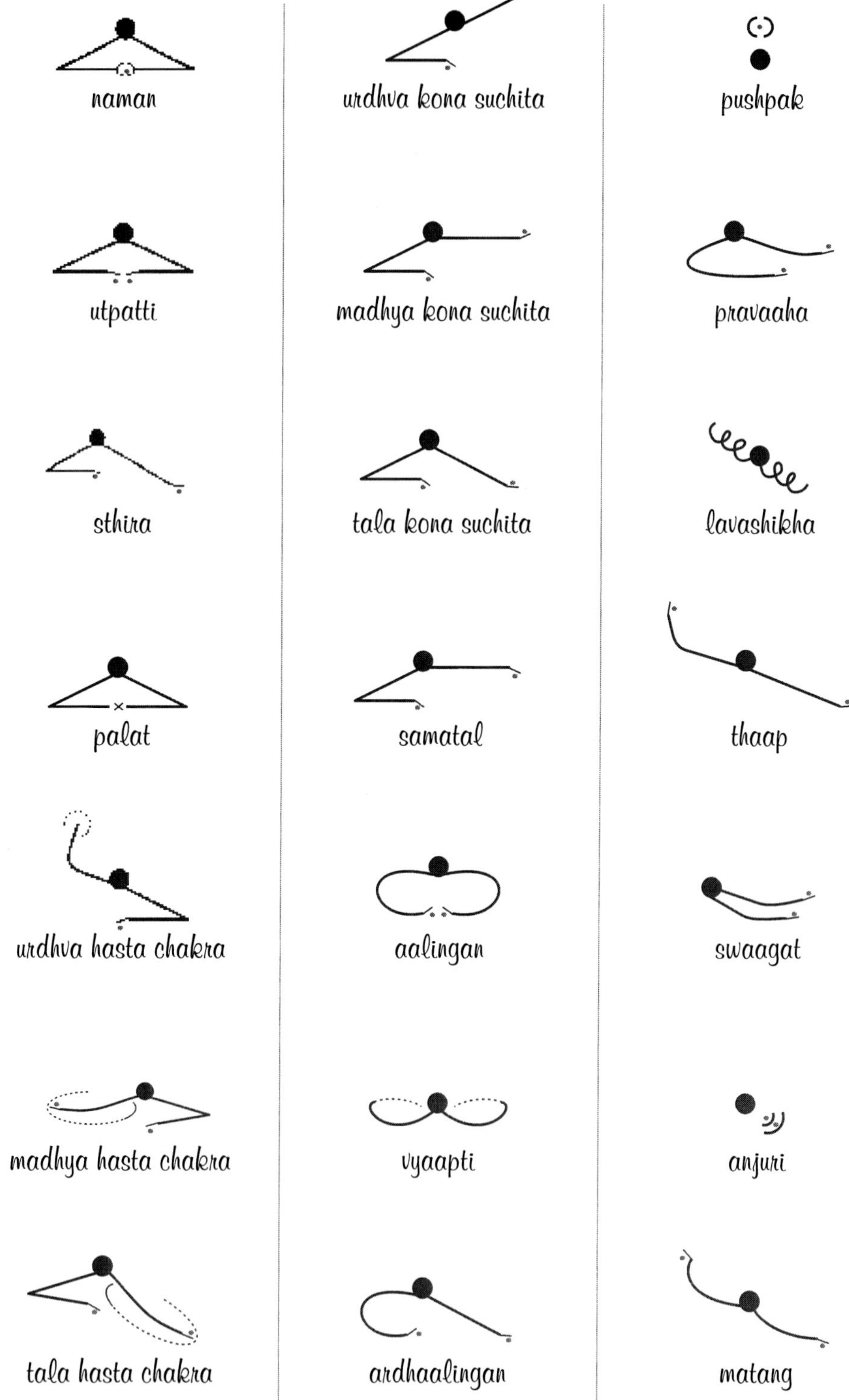

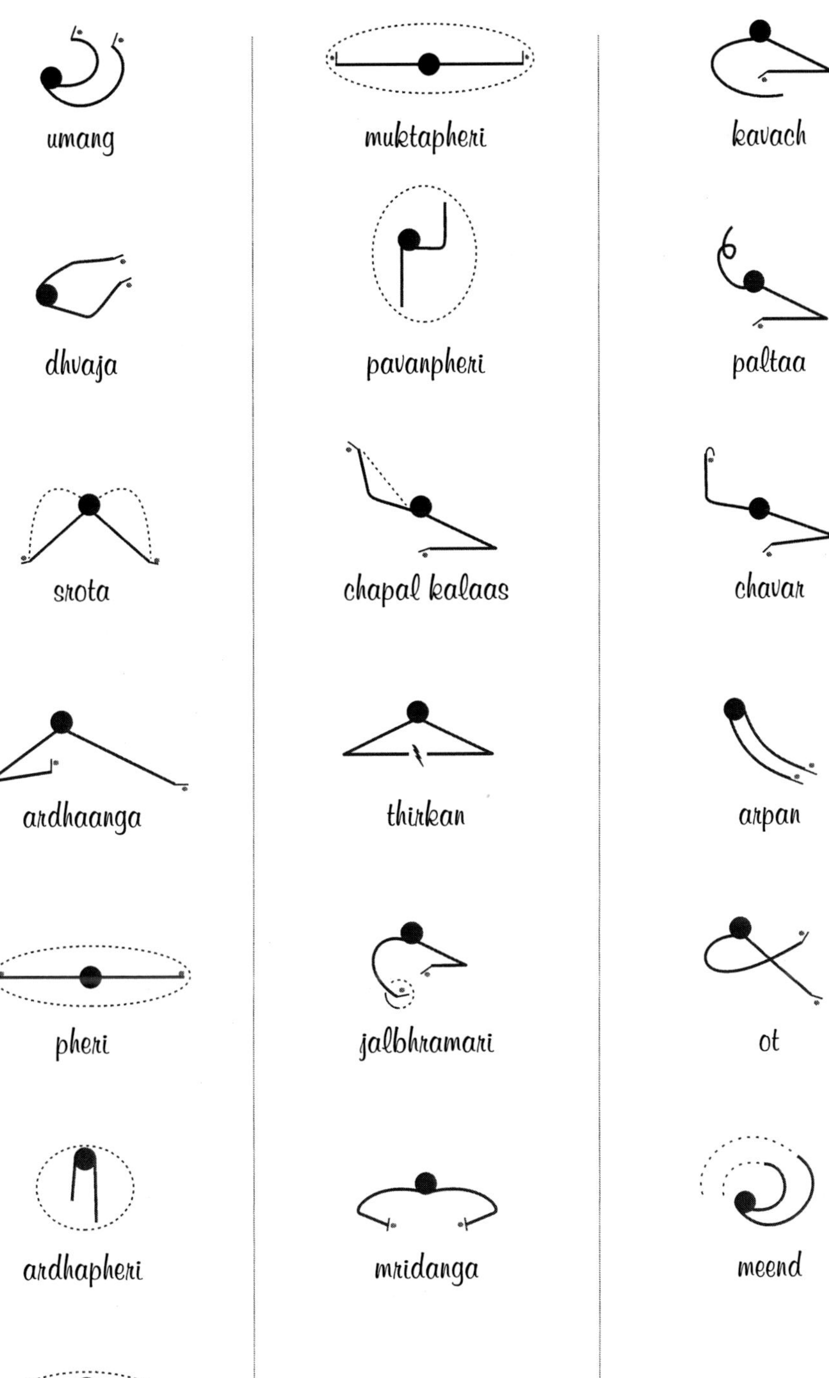

umang
dhvaja
srota
ardhaanga
pheri
ardhapheri
baddhapheri
muktapheri
pavanpheri
chapal kalaas
thirkan
jalbhramari
mridanga
jyoti
kavach
paltaa
chavar
arpan
ot
meend

Few simple exercises

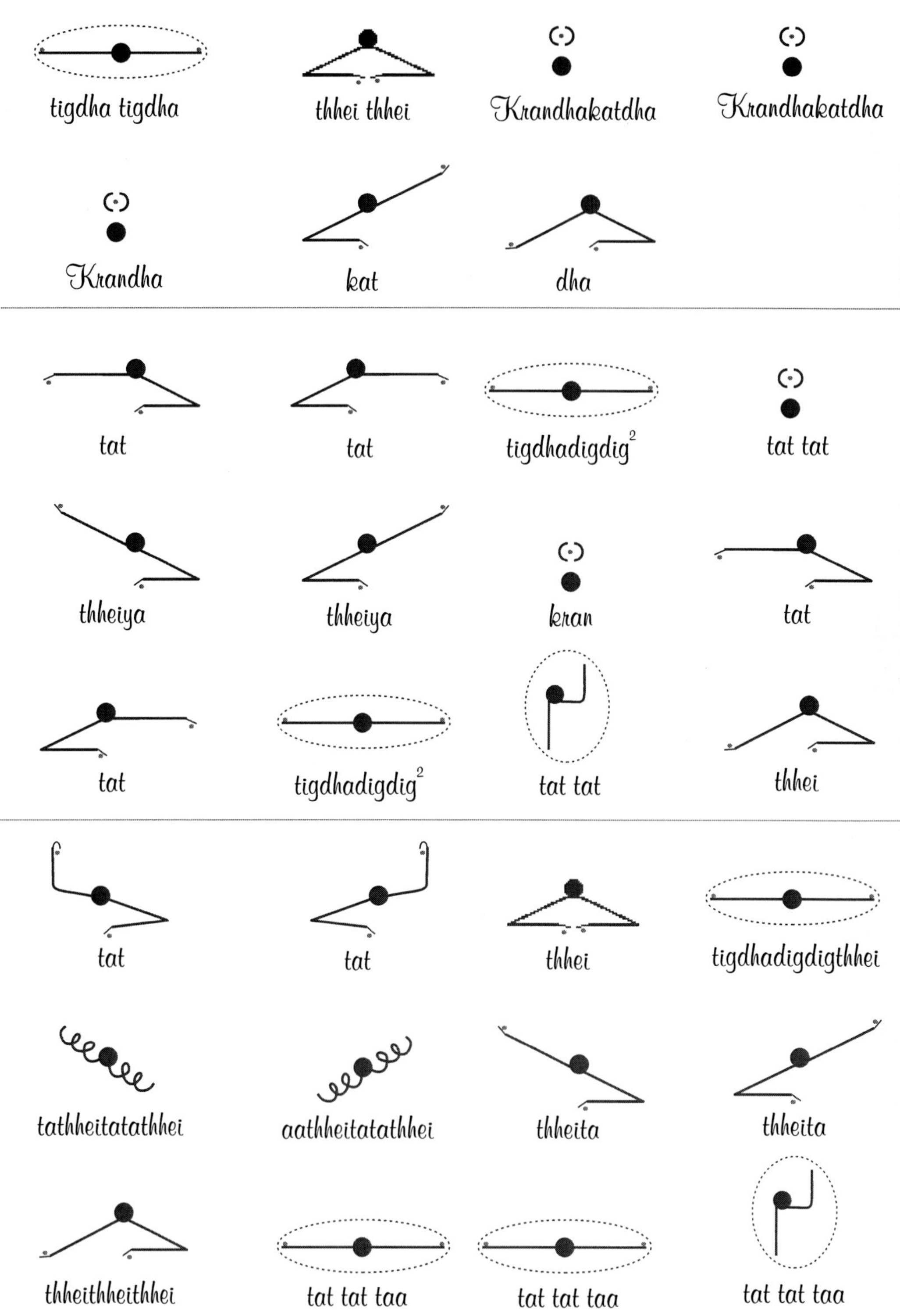

Feet positions

पद भंगिमा

ठोकर

thokar

सम

sama

अंगद

angad

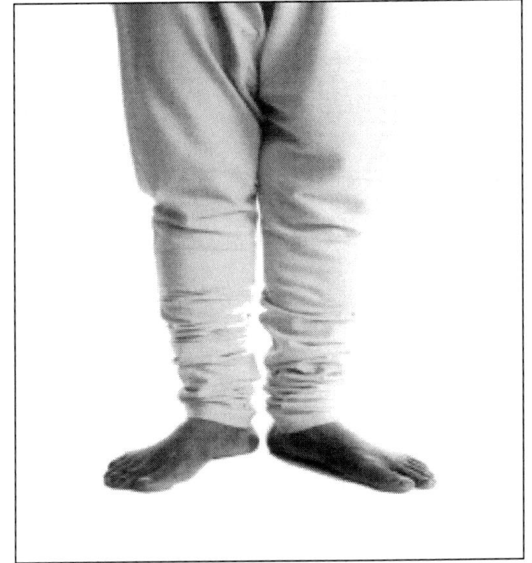

हनुमत

hanumat

कृष्ण

krishna

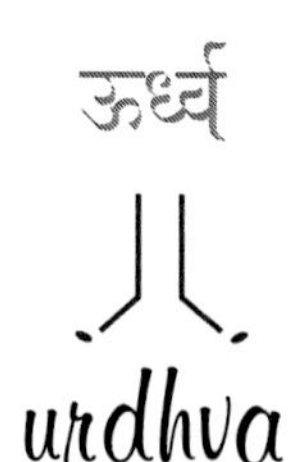

ऊर्ध्व

urdhva

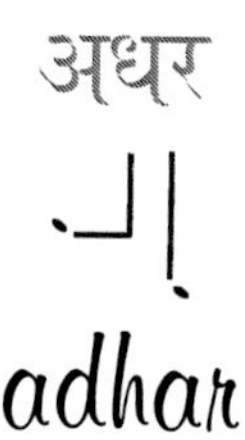

अधर

adhar

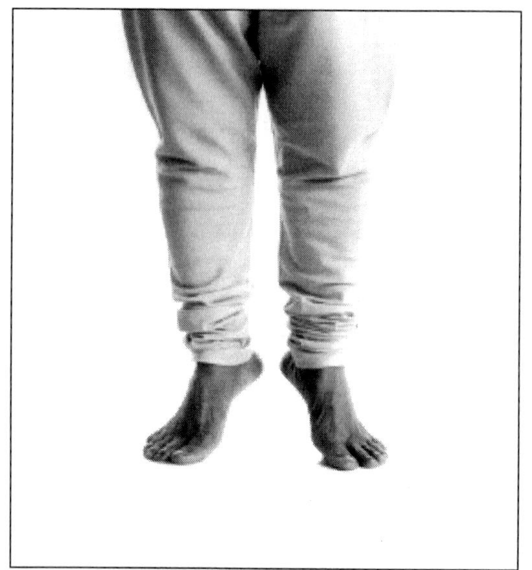

अर्धाघात

ardhaaghat

उछंग

uchhanga

ताण्डव

tandava

लास्य

lasya

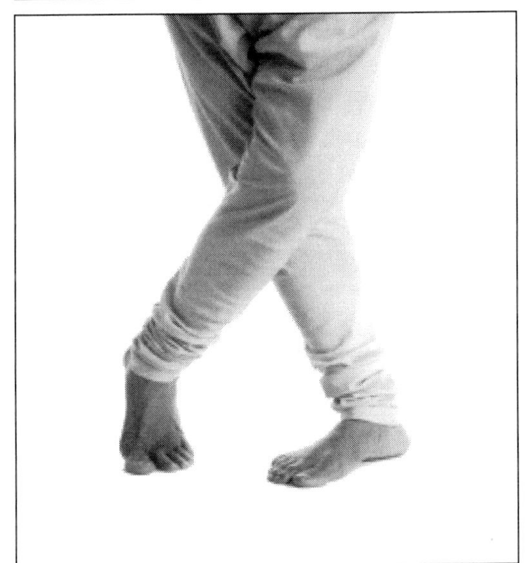

ललित

lalita

उड़ान

udaan

Notation symbols (feet)

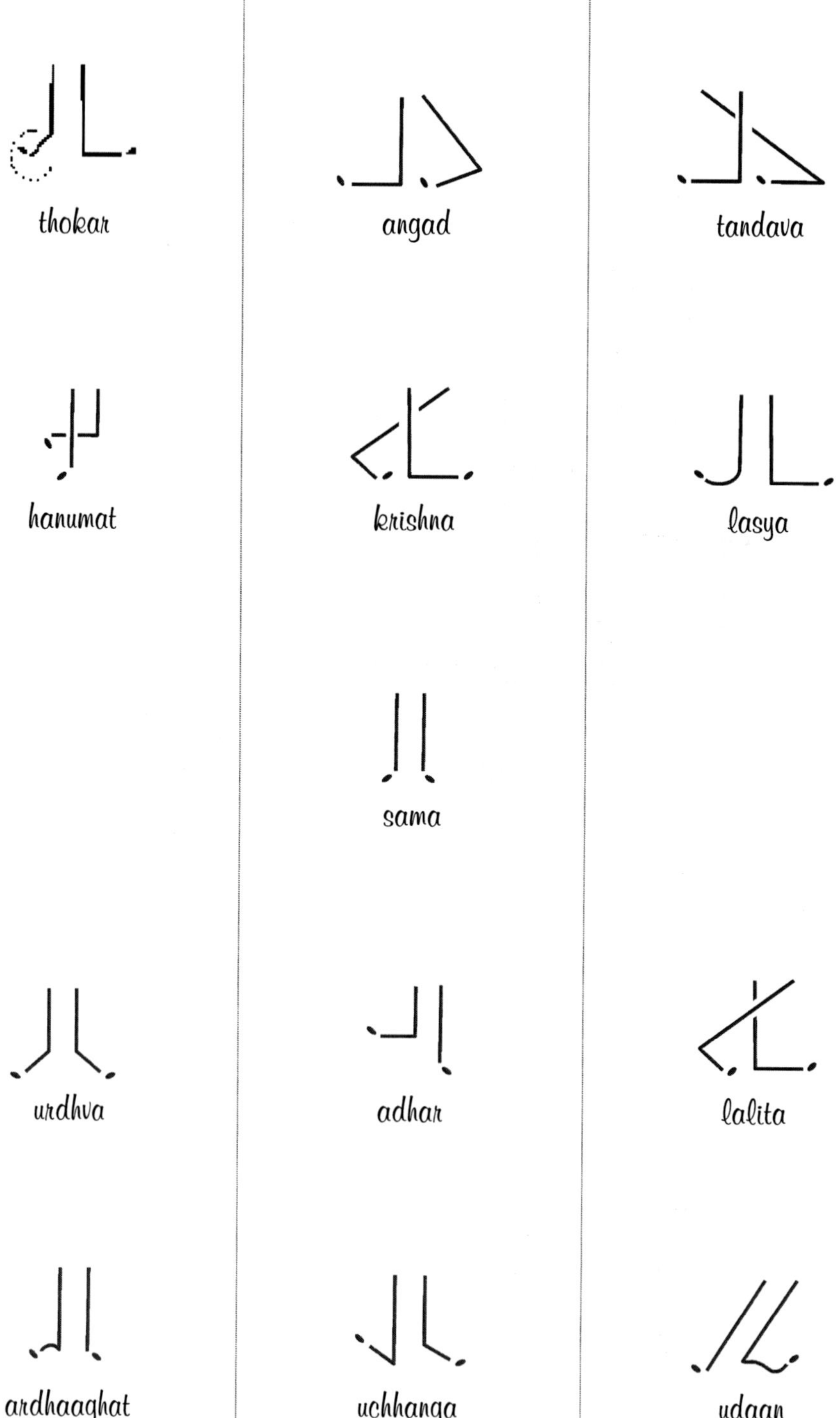

Stances

थाट

Finishing positions

सम

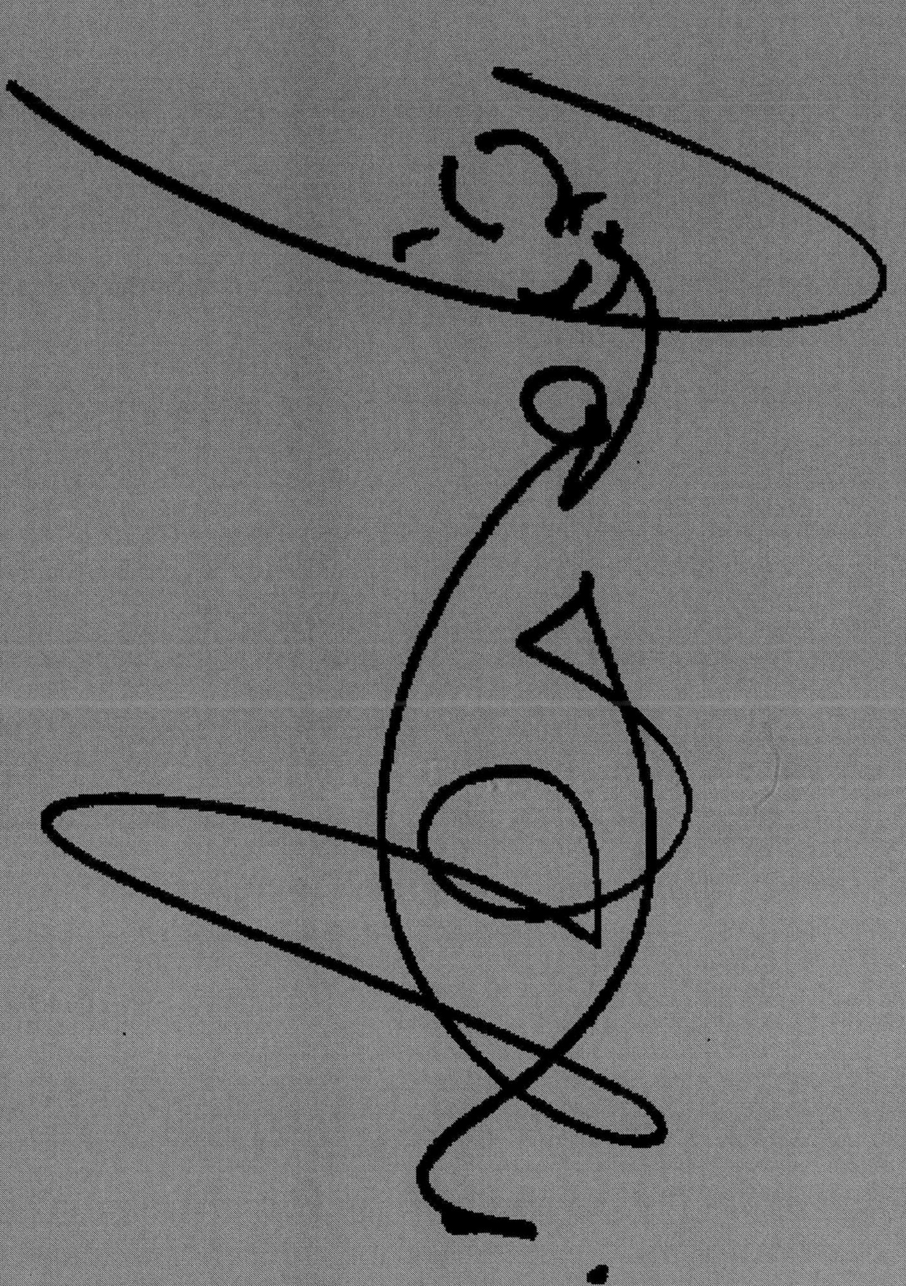

Repertoire

(The standard chronology of presentation)

Invocation

A prayer/An offering in praise of Guru/Any Deity/Nature/5 Elements etc. This could be a Vandana/Aradhana/Stuti/Shloka/Kirtan/Pada....

Vilambit Laya विलम्बित लय

Compositions in slow speed in any chosen Tala - most popularly Teen tala 16 beat cycle.

Upaj उपज

Brief patterns of footwork, spontaneously created within the Tala structure.

Thaat थाट

Holding the body in a particular dancing stance, while making very subtle movements of eyebrows, eyes, neck, wrist and upper torso.

Uthaan उठान

Small nimble rhythmic compositions which finish with an accent on 'sum', mostly ending with a Thaat.

Aamad आमद

Rhythmic compositions involving only the syllables 'Ta thei tat', and using slow graceful movements.

The above aspects establish the slow, contained movements and stances, unfolding the grace and fluidity in the form of the dance and the style of the dancer. The speed of the Tala starts from very slow pace, gradually increasing, to move towards medium pace.

Madhya Laya मध्य लय

Whereas there is no fixed pace to determine the exact speed of each 'Laya', this is a relative factor depending on the control of each dancer. However theoretically, and even as it is universally understood, Madhya Laya should be double speed of Vilambit, and Druta Laya should be a further double speed from Madhya. The dancer should be able to control these 3 speeds at ease without losing command on feet, body, hand movements and tal.

Tukra/Tora टुकड़ा/तोड़ा

Small phrases of rhythmic compositions performed with the entire body (i.e. feet, hands, torso, eyes etc.).

There are a few distinctive categories:

Natwari - using the syllable kran, tram

Tatkar - using the syllables of tatkar only (i.e. Ta Thei Tat, tigdha dig, thei).

Sangeet - using the syllable thhung, lung, thho

Parmelu - using several types of syllables, also imitation of nature sounds e..g. kukku, jhijhi, jhanak, thharra

Tihai तिहाई

Rhythmic phrases / patterns repeated three times mostly executed through feet

Druta Laya द्रुत लय

Compositions in fast speed.

Gat Nikas गत निकास

This is the most elegant, graceful aspect where a meaningful or abstract dancing stance is held and then the dancer moves in stylized walk or gait. A few typical ones Sidhi, Bansuri (flute) Rukhsaar (cheek), Ghunghat (veil), Aanchal (the saree end), Chhapka (a hair adornment) Mayur (peacock), Aalingan (embrace)

Gat Bhava गत भाव

An extension of Gat Nikas, where a story is enacted using the gesture language and facial expressions (without the help of words). Common ones - Panghat (fetching water from well), Chheda (to tease or play pranks), Makhan Chori (stealing butter milk), Holi (colour festival), Kaliya Daman (Krishna slaying the poisonous serpent king), Goverdhan Leela (Krishna lifting the mountain).

Paran परन

Rhythmic phrases composed of only Pakhawaj syllables (bols) executed with vigor and virtuosity.

Footwork

Long patterns of rhythmic phrases woven in succession. (Tatkar, Lari, Layabaant, Chalan, Jugalbandi.....)

Certain special items which are also interspersed:

Tarana तराना

A special musical composition set in a particular Raga, using the terms-derena, tanome, dira dira dim.

Thumri ठुमरी

A poetic composition mostly highlighting love, playfulness, longing, beauty. An intense piece of abhinaya.

Bhajan भजन

Offering obeisance, through a devotional composition in praise of some diety

Gazal ग़ज़ल

Expressing an urdu poetry with a feel of sensuousness, pathos or submission

Kavitta कवित्त

Portraying poetic compositions which are more descriptive or dramatic.

Chaturang चतुरंग

A musical composition having four aspects - lyrics, solfa notes (sargam), rhythmic phrases and tarana syllables.

Glossary of commonly used terms

Matra मात्रा	–	Beat (unit of measuring duration of a tal)
Tal ताल	–	Timecycle (Cyclic arrangement of beats to measure time).
Sum सम	–	First beat of a Tala which is usually most accented.
Tali ताली	–	Clap (Accent)
Khali खाली	–	Blank beat (Negative accent)
Bol बोल	–	Syllables
Theka ठेका	–	Rhythmic arrangement of syllables of any taal played on the drum.
Nagma/Lahra नगमा/लहरा	–	Melodic phrase which supports the rhythmic structure of any tala
Gati गती	–	Speed
Laya लय	–	Tempo (The gap between two strokes determines this) Three stages are : Vilambit - Slow, Madhya-Medium, Druta-Fast
Chhand छन्द	–	Symmetric and regular rhythm
Ginti गिनती	–	Counting (numerical patterns)
Bedam बेदम	–	Without pause or gap in the rhythmic structure
Adi आड़ी	–	Slant (converting 4-4 measure into 3 against 4 beats)
Kuwadi कुआड़ी	–	Converting 3-3 measure into 3-2 measure.

Jati जाती – The arrangement of syllables (bol) against the number of beats (matra), in measuring the musical time. Five main varieties are:

Chatusra चतुश्र - four in one matra; Tisra तिश्र - three in one matra; Khanda खण्ड - five in one matra; Misra मिश्र - seven in one matra; Sankirna संकीर्ण - nine in one matra.

Yati यती – The imaginative shape formed by the arrangement of bols in any rhythmic composition. Five popular varieties are:

Samaa समा - Even format

Srotogataa श्रोतगता - Narrow to broad

Pipilikaa पिपिलिका - Heavy on both ends, light in middle

Gopucchaa गौपुच्छा - Tapering

Mridangaa मृदंगा - Small at the ends, broad in centre

Layakari लयकारी – Rhythmic Interplay

Chakkardar चक्करदार – Three times repeated

Zarab/Wazan ज़रब/वज़न – Stress, accent

Parhant पढ़ंत – To Recite

Nritta नृत्त – Non-interpretative (Abstract)

Nritya नृत्य – Interpretative (Expressive)

Natya नाट्य – Theatrical, dramatic

Abhinaya अभिनय – Communicating an idea or feeling. Four major varieties are:

Vaachika वाचिक - through words : Aangika आंगिक - through body : Aaharya आहार्य -

through adorments : Saatwika सात्विक - through contemplation, which thereby appears on face.

Mudra मुद्रा	–	Stylized hand gestures
Bhava भाव	–	To express or to become
Rasa रस	–	Sentiment
Panja पंजा	–	Toe
Edi एड़ी	–	Heel
Ardhaghat अर्धाघात	–	Side stroke of feet
Hatheli हथेली	–	Palm
Nazar नज़र	–	Glance
Kalas/Gatta कलास/गट्टा	–	Wrist movements
Bhrukuti भृकुटि	–	Eyebrows
Kasak कसक	–	Twist of the upper torso
Masak मसक	–	Movement of chest due to inhalation and exhalation.
Gardan ka dora गर्दन का डोरा	–	Subtle, sideways neck movements
Meend मींड	–	A circular movement overhead (connecting the space around).
Palta पलटा	–	Reverse (back and forth turns used during 'Gat')
Chal चाल	–	Gait, specialized walk
Loach/Lachak लोच/लचक	–	Grace
Andaz अंदाज़	–	Poise
Ada अदा	–	Style
Chakkar/Pheri चक्कर/फेरी	–	Pirouettes/spins